Quick Revision

KS3

Science

Brian Arnold

First published 2007
exclusively for WHSmith by
Hodder Murray, a member of the Hodder Headline group
338 Euston Road
London
NW1 3BH

Impression number   10 9 8 7 6 5 4 3 2 1
Year   2010 2009 2008 2007

A CIP record for this book is available from the British Library.

The right of Brian Arnold to be identified as the author of this work has been asserted by him.

Cover illustration by Sally Newton Illustrations.

Typeset by Starfish Design Editorial and Project Management Ltd

ISBN: 978 0 340 94308 3

Printed and bound in the UK by Hobbs the Printers Ltd.

Acid rain

Acid rain is formed when gases such as carbon dioxide, sulfur dioxide and nitrogen dioxide dissolve in rainwater. These gases are released into the atmosphere when fossil fuels are burned, for example in cars, factories and power stations. (Some sulfur dioxide comes from natural sources such as volcanoes.) Acid rain is damaging to the environment. It can kill plants (including trees), and pond and lake life. It reacts with rocks and metals and can cause damage to buildings and structures. To lessen the effects of acid rain, we must take steps to reduce the amounts of these chemicals being released into the atmosphere.

Acids, alkalis and bases

Acids, alkalis and bases are types of chemicals. **Acids** are found in fruits such as apples and oranges, and in vinegar and car batteries. **Alkalis** are **bases** that will dissolve in water. They are found in soap, oven cleaners, washing-up liquid and toothpaste. Bases and alkalis neutralise acids. For example, the sting of a bee is acidic and can be neutralised using an alkali such as bicarbonate of soda. The sting of a wasp is alkaline, and can be neutralised using a weak acid such as vinegar.

Acids and bases/alkalis react together chemically to form salts. Some reactions of acids are listed below:

1 **acid + base or alkali ⇒ salt + water**
   e.g. sulfuric acid + magnesium oxide ⇒ magnesium sulfate + water
   hydrochloric acid + sodium hydroxide ⇒ sodium chloride + water

2 **acid + metal ⇒ salt + hydrogen**
   e.g. nitric acid + magnesium ⇒ magnesium nitrate + hydrogen

3 **acid + carbonate ⇒ salt + carbon dioxide + water**
   e.g.
   hydrochloric acid + magnesium carbonate ⇒ magnesium chloride + carbon dioxide + water

We can use **indicators** to discover which substances are acidic and which are alkaline.

SEE ALSO Indicators, pH scale

Alternative sources of energy

Coal, oil and gas are non-renewable sources of energy. When they have been used up, they cannot be replaced. Wood is a renewable source of energy. It can be replaced. To slow down the rate at which coal, oil and gas are being used, we must use alternative sources of energy.

Wind energy
Moving air is used to drive wind turbines to generate electricity.

Hydroelectric energy
Water that is collected behind dams is used to drive turbines to generate electricity.

Tidal energy
At high tide, water is trapped behind a barrier. At low tide, the water is released through turbines and electricity is generated.

Solar energy
The Sun is the main source of energy for the Earth. Light energy from the Sun can be converted directly into electricity using solar cells. Solar panels can be built into the roofs of houses to absorb energy from the Sun to heat water.

Biomass
Biological material such as wood is called biomass. It can be burned to release its energy. Animal manure can be stored in a large tank, and the gas given off can be used as fuel.

Wave energy
The constant up-and-down motion of water waves can be converted into electrical energy.

Geothermal energy
Deep underground, the Earth is very hot. If cold water is pumped down through pipes, it returns to the surface as steam, which can then be used to generate electricity.

Blood

Blood carries:
- oxygen and digested food molecules to the cells in our bodies
- carbon dioxide and waste products away from these cells
- white blood cells around our bodies.

Blood is a mixture of:
- **red blood cells**, which carry oxygen from the lungs to all the cells of the body
- **white blood cells**, which help protect us from disease by killing invading microbes
- **platelets**, which form clots to stop bleeding
- **plasma**, a watery liquid that contains all the above cells and other important substances such as dissolved food molecules and salt.

Breathing

When you breathe in, your diaphragm moves downwards, your rib cage moves upwards and outwards and air is drawn into your lungs.

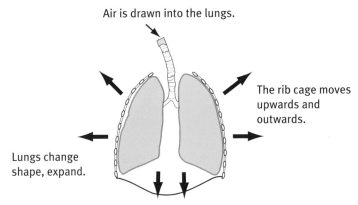

Air is drawn into the lungs.

The rib cage moves upwards and outwards.

Lungs change shape, expand.

The diaphragm moves downwards.

Continued overleaf

When you breathe out, your diaphragm moves upwards, and your rib cage moves downwards and inwards, pushing air out of your lungs.

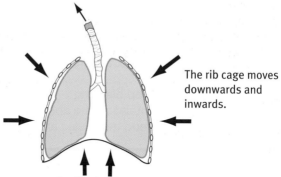

Air is pushed out of the lungs.

The rib cage moves downwards and inwards.

The diaphragm moves upwards.

In your lungs, oxygen passes through the thin walls of the air sacs (alveoli) into the blood, and carbon dioxide and some water passes out of the blood into the air sacs.

Gaseous exchange in an air sac

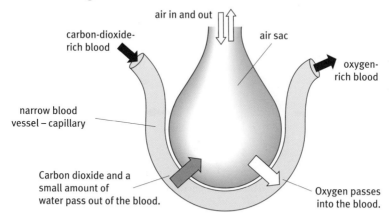

air in and out

carbon-dioxide-rich blood

air sac

oxygen-rich blood

narrow blood vessel – capillary

Carbon dioxide and a small amount of water pass out of the blood.

Oxygen passes into the blood.

Smoking damages the air sacs, making it more difficult for the oxygen to pass into the bloodstream. As a result, someone who smokes will get breathless more quickly when they exercise.

SEE ALSO Circulatory system

Cells

All living things are made from simple building blocks called cells. The chemical reactions necessary for life take place inside these cells.

Plant cells
A typical plant cell has:
- a **nucleus**, which controls the activities of the cell
- a semi-liquid called **cytoplasm**, where most of the reactions take place
- a **cell membrane**, which surrounds the cell and allows the flow of chemicals into and out of the cell
- **chloroplasts**, which absorb light energy so that the plant can make food (photosynthesis)
- a storage space called a **vacuole**, which is filled with a watery liquid
- a **cell wall**, which holds the plant cell together and gives the plant support and strength.

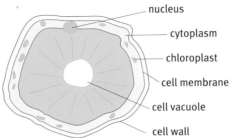

Animal cells
A typical animal cell has:
- a nucleus
- cytoplasm
- a cell membrane.

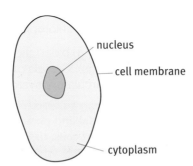

Note that an animal cell does not have a cell wall or chloroplasts. An animal cell may contain vacuoles, which would be small and widely spaced.

Continued overleaf

Some cells are adapted to do different jobs. These **specialised** cells have particular shapes and sizes.

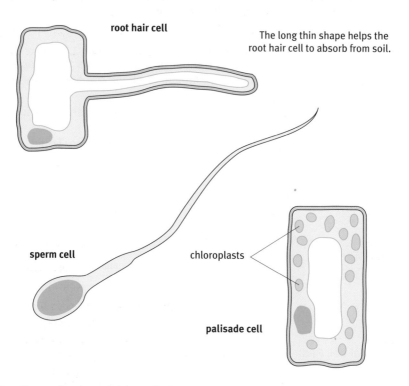

root hair cell

The long thin shape helps the root hair cell to absorb from soil.

sperm cell

chloroplasts

palisade cell

Root cells are long and thin to help them absorb nutrients and water.
Sperm cells have a tail to help them swim to the egg.
Palisade cells in a leaf contain lots of chloroplasts to absorb sunlight.

Groups of cells are called **tissues** (e.g. blood tissue, skin tissue). Groups of tissues form **organs** (e.g. eyes, lungs). Groups of organs working together form a **system** (e.g. digestive system, circulatory system).

SEE ALSO Photosynthesis, Plants, Respiration

Changes of state

If a **solid** is heated, its particles vibrate more vigorously until, at a particular temperature, its regular structure breaks apart and the particles are able to move around. The solid has changed into a **liquid**. It has **melted**.

The temperature at which this happens is called the **melting point** of that solid. If the liquid is cooled, the solid will re-form. The liquid will **solidify** or **freeze**.

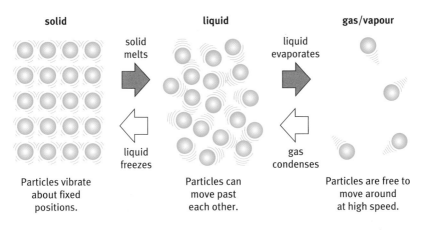

solid	liquid	gas/vapour
	solid melts → ← liquid freezes	liquid evaporates → ← gas condenses	

Particles vibrate about fixed positions.

Particles can move past each other.

Particles are free to move around at high speed.

If a liquid is heated, its particles will vibrate and move around even more vigorously until, at a particular temperature, the particles break away from each other and are completely free. The liquid has changed into a **gas**. It has **boiled**. The temperature at which this happens is called the **boiling point** of that liquid. If the gas is cooled, the liquid will re-form. The gas has **condensed**.
The melting point of ice is 0 °C; the boiling point of water is 100 °C.
Melting and boiling are **physical changes**.

SEE ALSO Physical changes

Chemical changes

A **chemical change** is one that produces a new substance and is difficult to reverse, such as baking a cake, burning paper or the setting of glue. There is no change in mass when a chemical change takes place. The atoms of the different substances taking part in the reaction are just combining in different ways. Virtually all materials are made through chemical reactions. In living organisms, these reactions take place within cells.

Chemical formulae

Compounds have a definite composition. We can show the composition of a compound using a chemical formula.

Name	Composition	Chemical formula
Water	Two hydrogen (H) atoms for each oxygen (O) atom	H_2O
Carbon dioxide	Two oxygen (O) atoms for each carbon (C) atom	CO_2
Sodium chloride (common salt)	One sodium (Na) atom for each chlorine (Cl) atom	NaCl
Copper oxide	One copper (Cu) atom for each oxygen (O) atom	CuO
Ammonia	One nitrogen (N) atom for three hydrogen (H) atoms	NH_3
Hydrochloric acid	One hydrogen (H) atom for each chlorine (Cl) atom	HCl
Calcium carbonate	One calcium (Ca) atom with one carbon (C) atom for three oxygen (O) atoms	$CaCO_3$

EXAM TIP

Learn the formulae of some of the most common compounds, e.g. water, carbon dioxide, common salt, etc.

Circuits

Most circuits contain a **cell** or **battery**, which acts like a pump moving the **current** around the circuit. If a larger current is needed, a cell with a larger **voltage** can be used, or two or more cells can be connected together.

cells and batteries

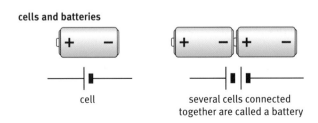

cell

several cells connected together are called a battery

Current can only flow around a circuit that is **complete** (i.e. there are no gaps). Current will not flow if the circuit is **incomplete**.

complete and incomplete circuits

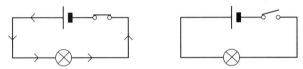

complete circuit – current flows   incomplete circuit – current does not flow

The size of the current that flows in the circuit depends on the voltage of the cell or battery and the type and number of components included in the circuit, for example the number of bulbs used.
We measure the size of the current flowing using an **ammeter**. We measure the voltage of a cell or battery using a **voltmeter**.

ammeters and voltmeters

This voltmeter measures the voltage of the battery.

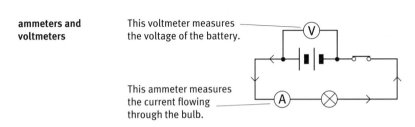

This ammeter measures the current flowing through the bulb.

Continued overleaf

Series and parallel circuits

In a **series circuit**, there is only one path for current to follow. There are no junctions. If one part of the circuit is turned off, the whole of the circuit is turned off.

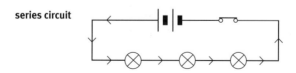

In a **parallel circuit**, there is more than one path for the current to follow. It is possible to turn off part of a parallel circuit and still have current flowing in other parts of the circuit.

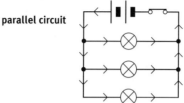

EXAM TIP

Learn the symbols for the most common components found in a circuit, for example, cell, battery, bulb, etc.

Circulatory system

- Blood is moved around the body by the pumping action of the heart.
- Blood that is rich in oxygen is pumped under high pressure through **arteries** to all parts of the body.
- Food molecules and oxygen pass out of the blood into cells through the walls of very narrow tubes called **capillaries**.
- Carbon dioxide and other waste products pass out of the cells into the capillaries.
- Blood that is rich in carbon dioxide returns to the heart under much lower pressure through tubes called **veins**.
- Arteries have thick elastic walls to withstand high pressure.
- Veins contain valves, which prevent the blood from flowing backwards.

The circulatory system

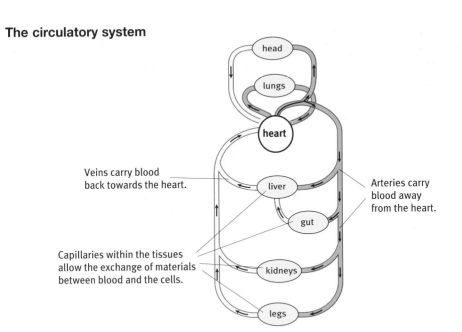

Veins carry blood back towards the heart.

Arteries carry blood away from the heart.

Capillaries within the tissues allow the exchange of materials between blood and the cells.

Remember: artery – away from the heart; vein – towards the heart.

Classification

More than 1 million different species live on Earth. To study them more easily, scientists have put them into groups that have similar features. This grouping is called **classification**. The five largest groups are called **kingdoms**. The two kingdoms we are most familiar with are called **plants** and **animals**. These groups can then be subdivided into even smaller groups. For example, the animal kingdom can be split into groups called the **vertebrates** and **invertebrates**. Vertebrates are animals with backbones such as birds, fish, mammals, reptiles and amphibians. Invertebrates are animals that have no backbones such as insects, spiders, worms and jellyfish.

Colour

If white light is shone through a glass prism, a band of colours called a **spectrum** is produced. This shows that white light is in fact a mixture of different colours of light. These are the colours of the rainbow. In order, they are red, orange, yellow, green, blue, indigo and violet.

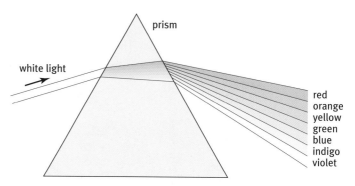

Coloured filters

Coloured filters are pieces of plastic or glass that allow some colours of light to pass through them but stop others. The colour that is allowed through is the colour of the filter, for example red filters allow only red light to pass through – all other colours are absorbed by the filter.

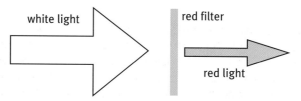

12

Coloured objects

We see an object when light reflected from it reaches our eyes. Red objects **reflect** red light and absorb all the other colours. Blue objects reflect just blue light, and green objects reflect just green light. White objects reflect all colours and absorb none. Black objects reflect no light. They absorb all colours.

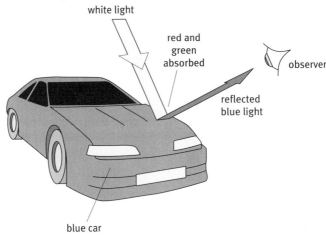

white light

red and green absorbed

observer

reflected blue light

blue car

Competition

All habitats have a limited amount of **resources** to support the plants and animals that live there. In order to survive, the animals and plants may have to **compete** for the resources.

Plants and trees
Plants and trees compete for water, air, sunlight, food and space. By adapting so that their needs are slightly different from those of their neighbours, they will have a better chance of survival. For example, some plants will grow tall so that they are exposed to lots of sunlight, and some will grow long roots to absorb water that is deep in the soil.

Animals
Within most habitats there are **predators** and **prey**. For predators to survive, they must be able to catch their prey. For example, tigers are successful predators because they are camouflaged, have strong leg muscles to run fast, and have long claws and sharp teeth to grab, hold and eat their prey. Prey such as antelope have developed good hearing and keen eyesight in order to survive. They are very agile and can run fast to help them escape a chasing predator.

Compounds and mixtures

Differences between compounds and mixtures

Mixtures

Often can be separated easily into the different substances, by filtering, dissolving, distilling, etc.

The properties of a mixture are usually similar to those of the substances that have been mixed. For example, if a mixture of iron filings and wood chippings is put in water, the filings will sink and the chippings will float.

Mixtures do not have a definite composition. The amount of each substance in the mixture can be changed.

Compounds

Usually extremely difficult to separate into the substances from which the compound was made.

The properties of a compound are usually different from those of the substances from which the compound is made. For example, egg, milk and flour can be baked to make a compound (a cake), which does not have the taste or properties of any of the ingredients.

Compounds have a definite composition. For example, water is a compound that has the chemical formula H_2O, which tells us that it contains two hydrogen atoms for every oxygen atom.

Current

An electric **current** is a flow of charge. As the charge flows through a cell or battery, it receives energy. The larger the voltage of the battery, the more energy the charge receives. This energy is then carried to the other components in the circuit, where it may be changed into different forms of energy, such as light, heat or sound energy.

Note: current is not 'used up' as it flows around a circuit. The current carries the energy, and it is the energy that is used.

EXAM TIP

It often helps to think of electric current moving through wires as being similar to water flowing through pipes. Electric current always flows from the positive side of a cell to the negative side.

SEE ALSO Circuits

Digestion

Digestion is the breaking down of large food molecules into simpler substances. These smaller molecules can then pass through the wall of the gut, dissolve in the bloodstream and be carried around the body. Chemicals called **enzymes** speed up the breakdown of large food molecules such as protein and starch.

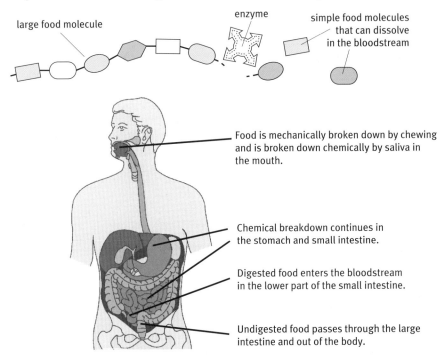

large food molecule

enzyme

simple food molecules that can dissolve in the bloodstream

Food is mechanically broken down by chewing and is broken down chemically by saliva in the mouth.

Chemical breakdown continues in the stomach and small intestine.

Digested food enters the bloodstream in the lower part of the small intestine.

Undigested food passes through the large intestine and out of the body.

Displacement reactions

In a displacement reaction, a more reactive metal will displace a less reactive metal from a compound such as a salt or oxide.

For example:
- iron + copper sulfate ⇒ iron sulfate + copper
  The more-reactive iron displaces the less-reactive copper.
- aluminium + iron oxide ⇒ aluminium oxide + iron
  The more-reactive aluminium displaces the less-reactive iron.

SEE ALSO Reactivity series

Dissolving

If you add some sugar to a cup of tea, the sugar seems to disappear. It has **dissolved** and formed a **solution**. The amount of a particular solid that can be dissolved in a liquid depends on a) the liquid being used and b) the temperature of the liquid. The higher the temperature of the liquid, the greater the amount of solid that can be dissolved. If sugar is added to a cup of tea until no more will dissolve, the solution formed is called a **saturated solution**.

Earth

The Earth is one of eight **planets** that orbit the Sun in our **solar system**. It takes the Earth one year to make one complete orbit of the Sun. As the Earth orbits the Sun, it also spins about its **axis** (an imaginary line that runs through the centre of the Earth from pole to pole). Because of the turning motion of the Earth, the Sun appears to rise in the east and set in the west. In the winter, the Sun's apparent daily journey follows a lower path across the sky.

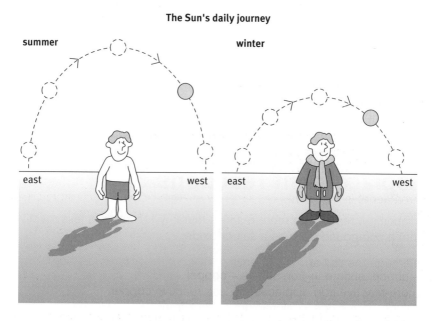

The Sun's daily journey

summer   winter

east   west   east   west

The spinning of the Earth also means that the stars in the night sky appear gradually to change position.

Day and night

As the Earth rotates, the areas of its surface that are facing the Sun receive light from it. For these places it is daytime. On the opposite side of the Earth, where there is no light from the Sun, it is night-time.

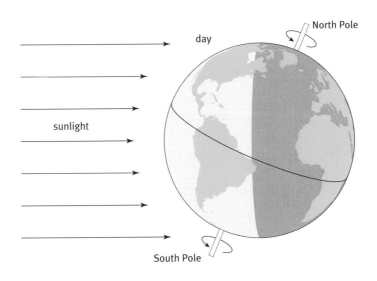

SEE ALSO Seasons, Solar system

Electromagnetism

An electromagnet is made by wrapping a wire around a piece of iron to create a coil. When current flows through the coil, the piece of iron becomes **magnetised**. When the current is turned off, the iron loses its magnetism. The strength of an electromagnet can be increased by a) increasing the current flowing through the coil and b) increasing the number of turns on the coil. The shape of the magnetic field around a coil is similar to the field around a bar magnet.

Electromagnets are useful because, unlike a permanent magnet, they can be switched on and off. For example, electromagnets are used in scrapyards to lift and drop cars, in electric bells and in relay switches.

Elements

An **element** is a pure substance that contains only one type of atom. It cannot be split into simpler substances. Gold and silver are elements. A ring made from pure gold contains only gold atoms. A ring made from pure silver contains only silver atoms.

The Periodic Table below shows some of the elements and their symbols.

1	2											3	4	5	6	7	0
							H Hydrogen										He Helium
Li Lithium	Be Beryllium											B Boron	C Carbon	N Nitrogen	O Oxygen	F Fluorine	Ne Neon
Na Sodium	Mg Magnesium											Al Aluminium	Si Silicon	P Phosphorus	S Sulfur	Cl Chlorine	Ar Argon
K Potassium	Ca Calcium	Sc Scandium	Ti Titanium	V Vanadium	Cr Chromium	Mn Manganese	Fe Iron	Co Cobalt	Ni Nickel	Cu Copper	Zn Zinc	Ga Gallium	Ge Germanium	As Arsenic	Se Selenium	Br Bromine	Kr Krypton
Rb Rubidium	Sr Strontium	Y Yttrium	Zr Zirconium	Nb Niobium	Mo Molybdenum	Tc Technetium	Ru Ruthenium	Rh Rhodium	Pd Palladium	Ag Silver	Cd Cadmium	In Indium	Sn Tin	Sb Antimony	Te Tellurium	I Iodine	Xe Xenon
Cs Caesium	Ba Berium	La Lanthanum	Hf Hafnium	Ta Tantalum	W Tungsten	Re Rhenium	Os Osmium	Ir Iridium	Pt Platinum	Au Gold	Hg Mercury	Tl Thallium	Pb Lead	Bi Bismuth	Po Polonium	At Astatine	Rn Radon
Fr Francium	Ra Radium	Ac Actinium															

[ ] metals [ ] non-metals

Elements can be classified as being metals or non-metals by studying their chemical and physical properties.

SEE ALSO Metals

Energy

We need energy to live. We use energy to 'do' things. We need energy to work. There are several different types of energy:

- **heat** or **thermal** energy, for example, from a fire or match
- **light** energy, for example, from a torch or from the Sun
- **sound** energy, for example, from a radio
- **chemical** energy, for example, from food

- **electrical** energy, for example, from a battery
- **nuclear** energy from the centre of some atoms
- **kinetic** or **movement** energy – an object has this type of energy if it is moving, for example, running water, wind
- **potential** or **positional** energy – an object has this type of energy if it is strained like a catapult, or if it is in a 'high place'.

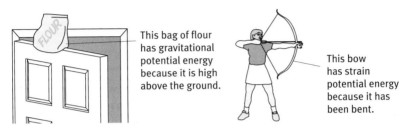

This bag of flour has gravitational potential energy because it is high above the ground.

This bow has strain potential energy because it has been bent.

Some forms of energy can be stored and used later, such as gravitational potential energy, strain or elastic energy, or chemical energy.

Energy transfer

When one type of energy is used to do something, that energy is not lost or used up – it is changed into a different type of energy. There is an **energy transfer**. This is known as the Law of Conservation of Energy. Examples of energy transfers are listed below.

Energy before transfer	Energy changer	Energy after transfer
electrical energy	loud speaker	sound energy
chemical energy (wax)	candle	heat and light energy
electrical energy	light bulb	light and heat energy
potential energy	catapult	kinetic energy
electrical energy	electric motor	kinetic energy
light energy	green plant	chemical energy

Although energy is never lost during an energy transfer, it often ends up in a less useful form. For example, the chemical energy in a match escapes into the air when the match is burned as heat, light and sound energy.

Food chains and food webs

Food chains show us what an animal eats and how energy is passed on. Plants are usually at the beginning of a food chain. Because they make their own food (by photosynthesis), they are called **producers**. Animals that obtain their energy by eating plants (e.g. cows and sheep) are called **primary consumers**. Animals that obtain their energy by eating the primary consumers (e.g. human beings) are called **secondary consumers**.

Animals that eat only plants (e.g. rabbits) are called **herbivores**. Animals that eat only meat (e.g. lions) are called **carnivores**.

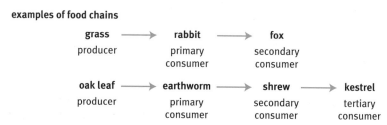

examples of food chains

We use **food pyramids** to show the numbers of producers and consumers in a food chain.

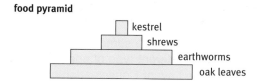

food pyramid

If a poison enters a food chain, its concentration becomes higher as it passes along the food chain. The concentration may be high enough to kill the animals at the top of the food pyramid.

It is unusual for a plant or animal to belong to just one food chain. A **food web** shows the relationships between members of several food chains.

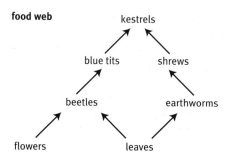

food web

Forces

There are many different types of forces, such as pushes, pulls, twists, squeezes, and so on. We measure the size of a force using a **newton meter**. A force of 1 N is approximately equal to the weight of a medium-sized apple.

There are several effects a force can have when applied to an object. It can:
- make the object start to move
- make the object move faster
- make the object slow down
- make the object stop
- change the direction in which the object is moving
- change the shape of the object.

If several forces are applied to an object and they cancel each other out, the forces are said to be **balanced**.

Friction
Friction is a force that tries to stop an object from moving or slipping. There will be a lot of friction between two rough surfaces as they try to slide over each other. If a lubricant such as oil or water is put between the surfaces, the friction is reduced.

If an accelerating force (one that is trying to make an object move faster) is balanced by the frictional force, the object will move at constant velocity.

EXAM TIP

Learn some examples of when the presence of friction is an advantage and when it is a disadvantage.

Fossil fuels

A **fuel** releases energy when it is burned. The most common fuels are coal, oil, gas and wood.
Coal, oil and gas are **fossil fuels**. They are formed from dead plants and animals that have been crushed under layers of mud for millions of years.
Wood is a **renewable** source of energy. More trees can be planted. Fossil fuels are **non-renewable** fuels. Once they have been used up, they cannot be replaced.

SEE ALSO Alternative sources of energy

Generating electricity

Most of the electrical energy we use in our homes is generated at a power station.

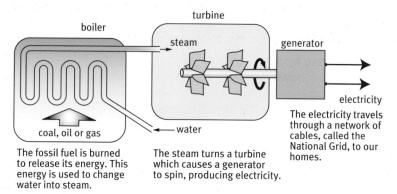

boiler

turbine

steam

generator

coal, oil or gas

water

electricity

The electricity travels through a network of cables, called the National Grid, to our homes.

The fossil fuel is burned to release its energy. This energy is used to change water into steam.

The steam turns a turbine which causes a generator to spin, producing electricity.

Burning fossil fuels increases the amount of carbon dioxide in the atmosphere, which contributes to global warming. It is therefore essential that we find alternative sources of energy.

Habitats and adaptation

A **habitat** is a place where a plant or animal lives, such as woodland, desert, a pond or the Arctic. The conditions of the habitat are called the **environment**. Plants and animals that live in a particular habitat are often adapted to survive in these conditions.

Cactuses can survive the hot, dry conditions found in deserts because:
- they store water in their stems
- they do not have leaves, so they lose less water by evaporation than a plant with leaves
- they have long roots to absorb water when it rains.

Camels are adapted to the desert environment in several different ways:
- they are able to store food (fat) in their humps
- they can drink (and store) large amounts of water
- they have large feet so that they are able to walk over the desert sands without sinking into it
- they have long eyelashes, which prevent the sand from being blown into their eyes.

Polar bears live in a very cold habitat. They are able to survive because:
- they have a thick fur coat, which helps to keep them warm
- they have a thick layer of fat beneath the fur – fat is an excellent insulator, and so reduces heat loss
- they can hibernate when conditions become really harsh.

Health and abuse

The human body is an incredible machine. To stay in good condition it needs a healthy balanced diet containing carbohydrates, protein, fat, minerals, vitamins, fibre and water. It also needs regular exercise. Abusing your body – for example, by smoking, drinking large quantities of alcohol or eating too much of the wrong kinds of foods – may cause permanent damage. Drugs taken under correct medical supervision can help people overcome injury or illness. Drugs taken without proper supervision can cause irreversible damage to major organs of the body such as the heart, liver and kidneys. Ultimately, the misuse of drugs can kill.

SEE ALSO Nutrition

Heat transfer

Heat energy can be transferred in three ways: by **conduction**, by **convection** and by **radiation**.

Conduction

The vibrations of the particles at the hot end of an object move heat to the cooler end.

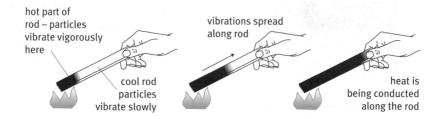

hot part of rod – particles vibrate vigorously here

cool rod particles vibrate slowly

vibrations spread along rod

heat is being conducted along the rod

Metals are good **conductors** of heat. Plastics and gases (e.g. fibreglass and polystyrene foam) are poor conductors of heat. They are **insulators** and are often used to prevent heat transfer.

Convection

Convection can only take place in a liquid or gas.

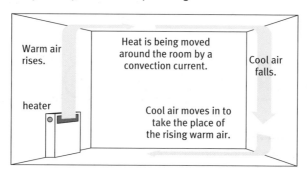

Warm air rises.

Heat is being moved around the room by a convection current.

Cool air falls.

heater

Cool air moves in to take the place of the rising warm air.

Radiation

Energy can also be transferred directly without the movement of any particles by **radiation**. Radiation is the movement of energy by rays or waves. Because it does not depend on the movement of particles, radiation can transfer energy across a vacuum. All the energy we receive from the Sun travels as radiation. Dark objects absorb radiation and become warmer. Light-coloured objects reflect radiation and remain cool. Heat will escape quickly from a house that is not insulated and, using our knowledge of how heat moves, we can take measures to reduce the rate at which it escapes.

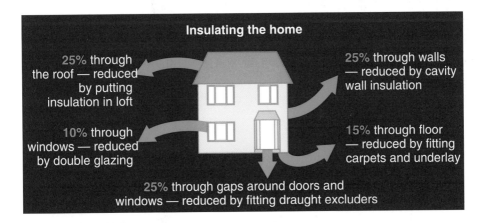

Insulating the home

25% through the roof — reduced by putting insulation in loft

25% through walls — reduced by cavity wall insulation

10% through windows — reduced by double glazing

15% through floor — reduced by fitting carpets and underlay

25% through gaps around doors and windows — reduced by fitting draught excluders

Indicators

Indicators such as **litmus** are coloured dyes that are used to show if a solution is **acidic**, **alkaline** or **neutral**. In acid solutions, litmus is red; in alkali solutions it is blue; and in neutral solutions it is purple.

Universal indicator is a mixture of dyes and can produce a range of colours. Its colour indicates how acid or alkaline a solution is.

universal indicator

← increasing acidity   increasing alkalinity →

RED	ORANGE	GREEN	BLUE	PURPLE
strong acid	weak acid	neutral solution	weak alkali	strong alkali

SEE ALSO **pH scale**

Joints and skeletons

Your body contains about 200 bones, which make up your skeleton. A skeleton:
- supports the body and gives it shape
- protects vital organs, for example, the rib cage protects the heart and lungs, and the skull protects the brain
- has joints to enable movement.

Continued overleaf

Two types of joints are hinge joints and ball-and-socket joints.
Hinge joints like the elbow and knee allow a pivoting motion in just one plane.

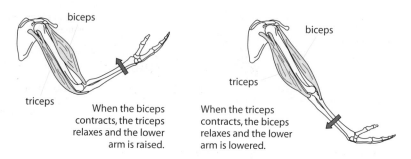

When the biceps contracts, the triceps relaxes and the lower arm is raised.

When the triceps contracts, the biceps relaxes and the lower arm is lowered.

Ball-and-socket joints like the hip and shoulder allow pivoting and rotation.

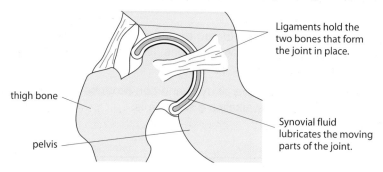

Ligaments hold the two bones that form the joint in place.

thigh bone

pelvis

Synovial fluid lubricates the moving parts of the joint.

Keys

Keys can be used to identify a plant or animal.

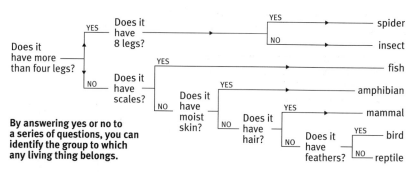

By answering yes or no to a series of questions, you can identify the group to which any living thing belongs.

Magnetic fields

Around a magnet is a magnetic field. We can see the shape of the magnetic field using iron filings.

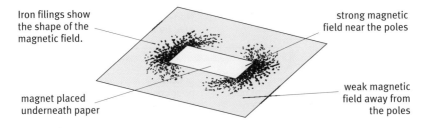

Iron filings show the shape of the magnetic field.

strong magnetic field near the poles

magnet placed underneath paper

weak magnetic field away from the poles

Magnets and magnetism

Magnetic materials such as iron or steel are attracted by magnets. **Non-magnetic** materials such as wood and plastic are not attracted by magnets. Magnetism is strongest at the **poles** of a magnet. Magnets usually have two poles, a **north pole** and a **south pole**.

If a bar magnet is suspended so that it is free to rotate, it will come to rest so that its north pole is pointing northwards and its south pole is pointing southwards. The bar magnet is behaving like a compass.

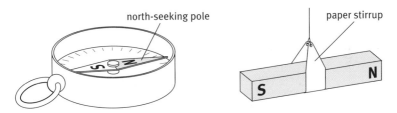

north-seeking pole

paper stirrup

If two similar poles are placed next to each other, they **repel**.
If two opposite poles are placed next to each other, they **attract**.

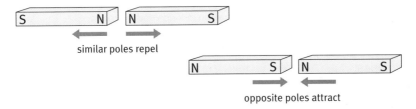

similar poles repel

opposite poles attract

Metals

Metals and non-metals

All elements can be classified as metals or non-metals. The group they belong to depends on their physical and chemical properties.

Property	Metals	Non-metals
state	all are solid (apart from mercury)	may be solid, liquid or gas
appearance	mostly shiny	very varied
strength	strong or very strong	generally weak
melting point	generally high	generally low
conduction	good conductor of both heat and electricity	poor conductor of both heat and electricity
density	mostly high	generally low
ductility	ductile (i.e. are able to be shaped into threads)	not ductile – these solids tend to be brittle
reaction with oxygen	form oxides that are basic	form oxides that are acidic

Chemical reactions with oxygen, water and acid

Reactions between metals and oxygen

Metal	Reaction with oxygen
sodium	Burns vigorously with a bright-yellow flame to form a white powder, sodium peroxide.
magnesium ribbon	Needs heating well before it catches fire, and burns with a bright-white flame. A white powder, magnesium oxide, is produced by the reaction.
iron filings	Even with strong heating, the filings will not burn but they will glow brightly. A black powder, iron oxide, is produced by the reaction.
copper foil	Even with strong heating, only the outer surface of the copper foil reacts with the oxygen, to form a coating of copper oxide.

Reactions of metals with water

Metal	Reaction with water
sodium	Violent reaction, becoming so hot the sodium melts. Sodium hydroxide and hydrogen gas are produced by the reaction.
magnesium ribbon	Reacts slowly, forming magnesium hydroxide and hydrogen.
iron filings	React very slowly. Small amounts of iron oxide and hydrogen are produced over a period of days or weeks.
copper foil	Does not react with water.

Reactions of metals with acids

Metal	Reactions with acid, for example, hydrochloric acid (dilute)
sodium	Extremely violent reaction – too violent to carry out in the lab
magnesium ribbon	Vigorous reaction, producing magnesium chloride and hydrogen
iron filings	React slowly to produce iron chloride and hydrogen.
copper foil	Does not react with acid.

From these reactions you can confirm the positions of these four metals in the reactivity series.

SEE ALSO Reactivity series

Moments

Sometimes when you apply a force, it makes an object turn or rotate. This turning effect of a force is called a **moment**.

examples of moments

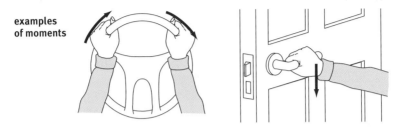

The size of a moment depends on a) the size of the force and b) the place where the force is applied. It can be calculated using the equation:
moment = force × distance.

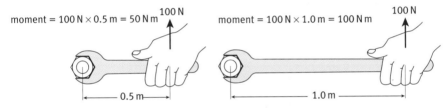

moment = 100 N × 0.5 m = 50 N m   100 N

moment = 100 N × 1.0 m = 100 N m   100 N

0.5 m

1.0 m

The longer the spanner, the larger the moment.

Balanced moments

If the see-saw in the diagram below balances, then the moment trying to turn it clockwise must be equal to the moment trying to turn it anticlockwise.

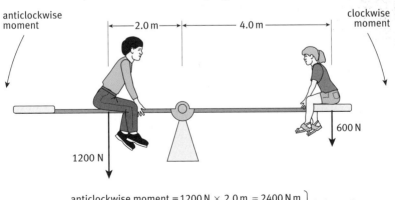

anticlockwise moment   clockwise moment

2.0 m   4.0 m

600 N

1200 N

anticlockwise moment = 1200 N × 2.0 m = 2400 N m ⎫
clockwise moment = 600 N × 4.0 m = 2400 N m ⎬ balanced
⎭

Nutrition

We all need food for energy and growth. The kind of food you eat and the amount of food you eat affects your health.

There are seven main components of food:

- **carbohydrates** – energy-giving foods, such as bread, rice, potatoes, pasta and sugar
- **fats** – also energy-giving foods, but they release the energy more slowly, for example, butter, margarine, fatty meats
- **proteins** – body-building foods, such as meat, cheese, eggs and fish
- **minerals** – simple chemicals that our bodies need to work properly, for example, calcium is needed for strong bones and teeth
- **vitamins** – more complicated chemicals that the cells of our bodies need to work properly; for example, vitamin A helps us to see at night and keeps our skin moist and healthy; vitamin D is needed to make bones strong
- **fibre** – helps to keep the digestive system clean and healthy; wholemeal bread and most vegetables contain lots of fibre
- **water** – needed to carry different materials around the body; your body is almost two-thirds water.

pH scale

Scientists use the pH scale to indicate the strength of an acid or alkali.
- A neutral solution has a pH value of 7.
- An acidic solution has a pH value less than 7.
- An alkaline solution has a pH value greater than 7 (up to a maximum of 14).

pH scale

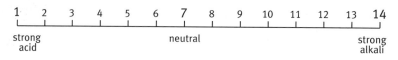

Photosynthesis

Most plants make their own food (glucose) by a process called **photosynthesis**, which takes place in the green parts of the plant (usually the leaves). Chlorophyll (the substance that gives leaves their green colour) absorbs light energy so that the plant can make food. The reaction that produces this food is:

sunlight

water + carbon dioxide $\Rightarrow$ glucose + oxygen

The glucose may be used immediately to produce the energy the plant needs to live (respiration), or it may be changed into more complicated substances such as starch, which is stored food, or cellulose, which is used to make cell walls.

Learn the word equation for photosynthesis.

SEE ALSO **Plants, Respiration**

EXAM TIP

Physical changes

A physical change is:
- usually easy to reverse
- a change in which no new substance is created
- a change in which the mass of the object/substance stays the same.

Examples of physical changes include:
- melting
- boiling
- dissolving
- thermal expansion and contraction.

Plants

During the daytime when there is sunlight, **photosynthesis** takes place in the green parts of a plant (usually the leaves). Some of the glucose produced is used straight away to produce the energy the plant needs to live (respiration). Some of the glucose is changed to starch and is stored for later use.

Continued overleaf

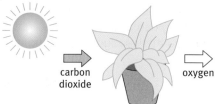

Some of the glucose produced by photosynthesis is stored by the plant for later use.

During the night there is no light, so plants use some of their stored food for energy.

respiration

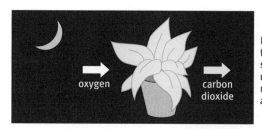

Photosynthesis does not take place when there is no sunlight. Stored food is used to provide the energy necessary for respiration at night.

The process by which plants release the energy stored in food is called **aerobic respiration**. The biological material they make as they grow is called **biomass**.

SEE ALSO Photosynthesis, Respiration

Pressure

If a force is concentrated onto a small area, it creates a large pressure. If the same force is spread out over a large area, it creates a much smaller pressure.

Larger area creates a smaller pressure.

Smaller area creates a greater pressure.

In the diagram on page 32, the man on the left is wearing snowshoes, so his weight is spread over a large area. He is therefore able to walk on top of the snow. His friend is not wearing snowshoes. His weight is concentrated onto a smaller area, creating a higher pressure. This higher pressure causes him to sink into the snow.

We can calculate the pressure created by a force using the equation:

$$\text{pressure} = \frac{\text{force}}{\text{area}}$$

We measure pressure in pascals (Pa) where $1\,\text{Pa} = 1\,\text{N/m}^2$.

For example, to calculate the pressure created when a woman weighing 500 N stands on a piece of wood of area $2\,\text{m}^2$:

$$\text{pressure} = \frac{\text{force}}{\text{area}} = \frac{500\,\text{N}}{2\,\text{m}^2} = 250\,\text{Pa}$$

Reactivity series

The reactivity series is a list of metals. The most reactive metals are at the top of the list. The least reactive metals are at the bottom.

Potassium (K)   **Most reactive**
Sodium (Na)
Calcium (Ca)
Magnesium (Mg)
Aluminium (Al)
Zinc (Zn)
Iron (Fe)
Lead (Pb)
Copper (Cu)
Silver (Ag)
Gold (Au)   **Least reactive**

Use this sentence to help you remember the order of the metals in the series:
Poor **S**ally **C**an't **M**anage **A**ny **Z**eal **I**n **L**atin **C**os **S**he's **G**lum.

SEE ALSO Displacement reactions

Reflection

We see **luminous** objects such as the Sun, fires and lamps because they **emit** light. We see **non-luminous** objects because they **reflect** light.

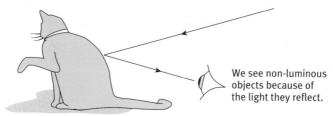

We see non-luminous objects because of the light they reflect.

Light travels in straight lines. When a ray of light strikes a flat, smooth surface, it is reflected so that the angle of incidence is equal to the angle of reflection.

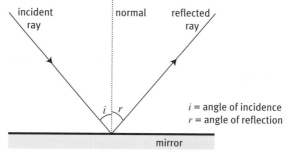

incident ray   normal   reflected ray

i = angle of incidence
r = angle of reflection

mirror

A smooth surface looks shiny because the rays of light that reach it from the light source are all reflected in the same direction, so lots of light rays enter your eyes. A rough surface looks dull because the rays of light are being scattered, so fewer of them enter your eyes.

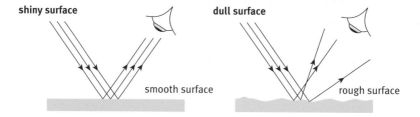

shiny surface

smooth surface

dull surface

rough surface

Refraction

Light can travel through many different transparent materials, such as air, water and glass. These materials are called **media**. When a ray of light crosses the boundary between two media, its speed and the direction in which it is travelling may change. This change in direction is called **refraction**.

When a ray of light travels from air into glass or water, it slows down and bends towards the normal.

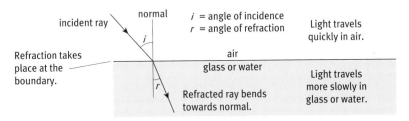

When a ray of light travels from glass or water to air, it speeds up and bends away from the normal.

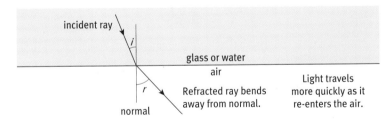

Because we expect light to travel in straight lines, this bending can sometimes produce optical illusions.

The bending of the light as it leaves the water makes the pencil look bent.

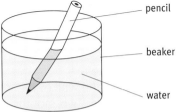

A ray that strikes a boundary at 90° passes straight through without changing its direction.

Reproduction (human)

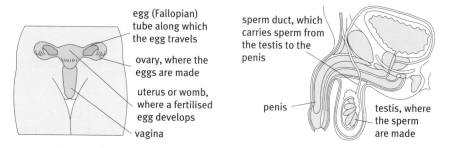

egg (Fallopian) tube along which the egg travels

ovary, where the eggs are made

uterus or womb, where a fertilised egg develops

vagina

sperm duct, which carries sperm from the testis to the penis

penis

testis, where the sperm are made

All human life begins with sexual reproduction. During sexual intercourse, sperm pass through the man's penis into the vagina of the woman. The sperm travel through the womb (uterus) and into the egg (Fallopian) tubes. If there is an egg (ovum) in one of the tubes, it may become fertilised.

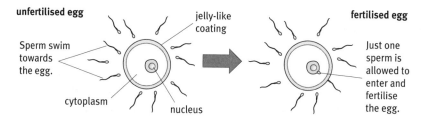

unfertilised egg

jelly-like coating

fertilised egg

Sperm swim towards the egg.

Just one sperm is allowed to enter and fertilise the egg.

cytoplasm

nucleus

Menstrual cycle

An ovum is released from one of a woman's ovaries approximately once every 28 days. The ovum travels along one of the egg tubes. If it is fertilised, it attaches itself to the wall of the womb where a lining has developed in readiness for the fertilised ovum. If the ovum is unfertilised, it and the lining of the womb pass through the vagina. This discharge of ovum and lining is commonly called 'having a period'. The whole process then begins again. This 28-day cycle is called the **menstrual cycle**.

Pregnancy

A fertilised ovum attached to the wall of the womb divides again and again, producing more and more cells. Two months after fertilisation, it begins to have some baby-like features – it has a face, arms, legs, fingers and toes. At this stage in its development it is called a **fetus**. The fetus is connected to the **placenta** by the **umbilical cord**. In the placenta the fetus's blood absorbs oxygen and food from the mother's blood and releases carbon dioxide and other waste products. The growth of the baby within the mother usually lasts 280 days, or about nine months.

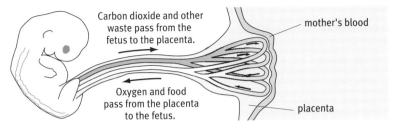

Carbon dioxide and other waste pass from the fetus to the placenta.

mother's blood

Oxygen and food pass from the placenta to the fetus.

placenta

Puberty

Children are unable to reproduce. Their reproductive organs are not yet ready to produce eggs (ova) and sperm. As the organs become mature, several other changes take place in their bodies. The time when these physical changes happen is called **puberty**.

Boys:
- voice becomes deeper
- hair grows on the face, chest and around the pubic region
- physique becomes more muscular.

Girls:
- breasts develop
- hair grows around the pubic region
- periods start.

At the same time that these physical changes are taking place, emotional changes also occur, such as becoming more self-conscious and more aware of the opposite sex. This period of change is called **adolescence**.

Respiration

All living things need energy to live. The process of obtaining this energy is called **respiration**. The chemical reaction that releases this energy is:

glucose + oxygen $\Rightarrow$ carbon dioxide + water + energy

Animals obtain glucose by digesting food. They obtain the oxygen they need from the air they breathe.

Plants make glucose by photosynthesis. They absorb the oxygen they need for respiration from the air through tiny pores in their leaves called stomata.

Learn the word equation for respiration.

EXAM TIP

Rock cycle

Within the crust of the Earth, rocks are being continuously created, destroyed and then re-created over a period of millions of years. This recycling of rocks is called the **rock cycle**.

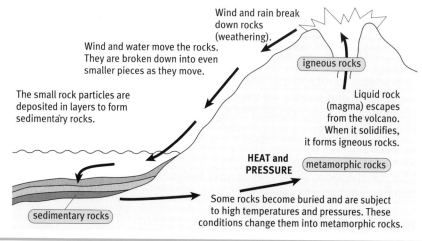

Wind and rain break down rocks (weathering).

Wind and water move the rocks. They are broken down into even smaller pieces as they move.

The small rock particles are deposited in layers to form sedimentary rocks.

igneous rocks

Liquid rock (magma) escapes from the volcano. When it solidifies, it forms igneous rocks.

HEAT and PRESSURE

metamorphic rocks

sedimentary rocks

Some rocks become buried and are subject to high temperatures and pressures. These conditions change them into metamorphic rocks.

Rocks

There are three main types of rock within the crust of the Earth. These are **igneous**, **sedimentary** and **metamorphic**.

Igneous rocks are formed when molten rocks cool and solidify. They are hard and crystalline. Examples of igneous rock are granite and basalt.

Sedimentary rocks are formed from small particles that settle out of water. Over a long period of time, these particles are squashed together by the weight of other particles being deposited on top of them. Because they are formed in this way, sedimentary rocks have a layered structure. They are soft and often contain fossils. Examples of sedimentary rocks are limestone and sandstone.

Metamorphic rocks are formed from igneous or sedimentary rocks that are heated and/or squashed by very high pressures. For example, when limestone is subject to high temperatures and pressures, it changes into marble. Most metamorphic rocks are very hard.

Satellites

The Moon orbits the Earth. It is a **natural satellite**. Many man-made objects also orbit the Earth. These are called **artificial satellites**.

We use artificial satellites:

- to observe events on the Earth, for example, weather satellites and 'spy' satellites
- for communications, such as radio, TV and mobile phones
- to look deep into outer space.

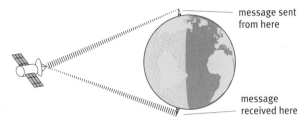

Radio waves travel in straight lines. To talk to someone on the other side of the Earth we use communication satellites.

message sent from here

message received here

Seasons

As the Earth travels around the Sun, we experience the changing seasons: spring to summer to autumn to winter. This happens because the **axis** (an imaginary line from pole to pole through the centre) of the Earth is tilted. When our part of the Earth is tilted towards the Sun, it is summer in the northern hemisphere and winter in the southern hemisphere. When our part of the Earth is tilted away from the Sun, it is winter in the northern hemisphere and summer in the southern hemisphere.

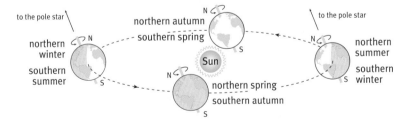

to the pole star

northern autumn
southern spring

northern winter
southern summer

to the pole star

northern summer
southern winter

Sun

northern spring
southern autumn

Tilting of the Earth causes the seasons. Spinning of the Earth causes day and night.

Separation

Mixtures can be separated in several different ways.

1 Filtration

This method can be used to separate a mixture such as sand and water.

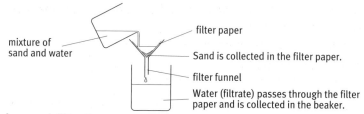

mixture of sand and water

filter paper

Sand is collected in the filter paper.

filter funnel

Water (filtrate) passes through the filter paper and is collected in the beaker.

2 Dissolving and filtration

This method can be used to separate a mixture such as sand and salt.

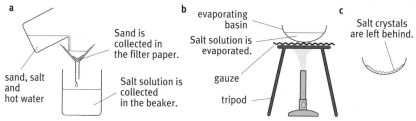

a sand, salt and hot water

Sand is collected in the filter paper.

Salt solution is collected in the beaker.

b evaporating basin

Salt solution is evaporated.

gauze

tripod

c Salt crystals are left behind.

3 Distillation

This method can be used to separate a mixture of two liquids that have different boiling points, or to separate and recover a liquid from a solution.
Alcohol can be separated from a mixture of water and alcohol by distillation. As the temperature of the mixture increases, the alcohol, which has the lower boiling point, begins to boil. As the vapour travels along the condenser, it is cooled and changes back into a liquid (**condenses**). At the end of the process, the liquid with the higher boiling point is left in the flask.

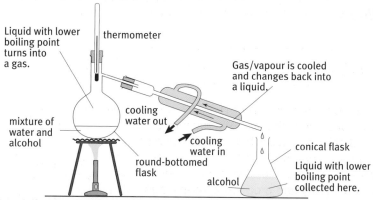

Liquid with lower boiling point turns into a gas.

thermometer

Gas/vapour is cooled and changes back into a liquid.

mixture of water and alcohol

cooling water out

cooling water in

round-bottomed flask

alcohol

conical flask

Liquid with lower boiling point collected here.

4 Chromatography

This method is used to separate a mixture of two or more liquids, such as two dyes mixed together to produce a particular colour of ink. A drop of ink is placed on some filter paper, which is stood in water in a beaker.

As the water rises up the filter paper, the different dyes in the ink travel different distances and are therefore separated.

Solar system

Our solar system consists of one star – the Sun – and eight planets and their moons. The planets, starting with the one nearest the Sun, are Mercury, Venus, Earth, Mars, Jupiter, Saturn, Uranus and Neptune. (Pluto is now regarded as a 'dwarf' planet.)

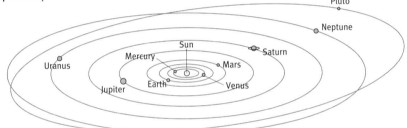

All the planets move around the Sun in **elliptical** (squashed-circle) orbits. The solar system is held together by the forces of gravity. These forces control the positions and motions of the planets. The planets closest to the Sun experience the largest forces.

EXAM TIP

This sentence will help you remember the planets in the correct order.
<u>M</u>any <u>V</u>ery <u>E</u>nergetic <u>M</u>en <u>J</u>og <u>S</u>lowly <u>U</u>p to <u>N</u>ewport <u>P</u>agnell.

Sound

All sounds begin with an object vibrating, for example, the strings of a guitar, the skin of a drum or the wings of a bee. Small objects, such as the strings on a violin, vibrate quickly and produce high-pitched notes. Large objects, such as the strings on a double bass, vibrate more slowly and produce lower-pitched notes.

high-pitched sound

low-pitched sound

Continued overleaf

41

Loudness of sounds

The larger the amplitude of vibration of an object, the louder the sound it produces. Exposing your ears to loud sounds for long periods of time can lead to temporary or even permanent deafness.

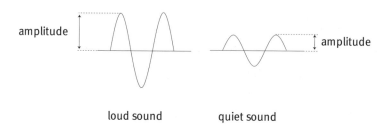

loud sound   quiet sound

Hearing range

There are some sounds that have such a high pitch or such a low pitch that they cannot be heard by human beings. The range of frequencies we can hear is called our **hearing range**. The size of the hearing range varies from person to person but, in general, older people have a narrower hearing range.

EXAM TIP

Learn the shapes of the waves produced by the different types of sounds.

Sound waves

Sounds travel from the source to our ears as sound waves. These waves travel through the air at approximately 340 m/s. Light waves travel much faster than sound waves. This is why when lightning strikes we see the flash first and hear the thunder some time later.

Sound waves can travel through solids, liquids and gases but they cannot travel through a vacuum.

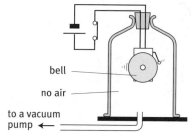

bell

no air

to a vacuum pump ←

When all the air is pumped out no sound can be heard, even though the bell is seen to be vibrating. Sound waves cannot travel through a vacuum, but light waves can.

Speed

The speed of an object tells us how quickly it is moving. Speed is usually measured in m/s (metres per second) or km/h (kilometres per hour). We can calculate the speed of an object using the equation:

$$speed = \frac{distance}{time}$$

For example, if an Olympic athlete runs 400 m in 40 s, his average speed is:

$$speed = \frac{distance}{time} = \frac{400\,m}{40\,s} = 10\,m/s$$

If an object is increasing its speed, it is **accelerating**.
If an object is decreasing its speed, it is **decelerating**.

Stars

The Sun is our nearest star. It is at the centre of our solar system. Stars are **luminous** objects. They emit light. Other bodies in our solar system, such as the moon and the planets, are **non-luminous** objects. We see them because they reflect light from the Sun.

Small groups of stars are called **constellations**. Many can be seen in the night sky with the naked eye and have names and shapes that you may know, such as the Plough, Capricorn, Cancer and Orion.

Very large groups of stars and constellations are called **galaxies**. The galaxy we live in contains about 200 million stars and is called the Milky Way.

the Plough constellation

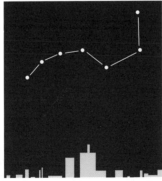

The brightness of a star depends upon a) the type of star it is and b) its distance from the Earth. The further away it is from the Earth, the dimmer/fainter it will appear in the night sky.

States of matter

There are three states of matter: solid, liquid and gas. All matter is made up of tiny particles. The arrangement of these particles gives solids, liquids and gases their different properties.

	solids	liquids	gases
spacing of particles	very close together	close together	very widely spaced
forces between particles	strong forces hold the structure together	slightly weaker forces than solids	no forces of attraction
movement of particles	vibrate about a fixed position	able to slide past each other	able to move at high speeds in all directions
typical properties	fixed shape; can support things	able to flow; a liquid will take the shape of the container into which it is poured	a gas will fill any container into which it is released; can be squashed

Diffusion

The particles of a liquid or gas are able to move around and mix. This mixing is called **diffusion**.

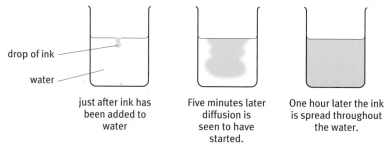

drop of ink

water

just after ink has been added to water

Five minutes later diffusion is seen to have started.

One hour later the ink is spread throughout the water.

Gas pressure

Gas particles move very quickly, continually rebounding from the walls of the container in which they are placed. These collisions create the pressure inside a gas. If you pump more air particles into a tyre, there are more collisions and so the pressure inside the tyre increases.

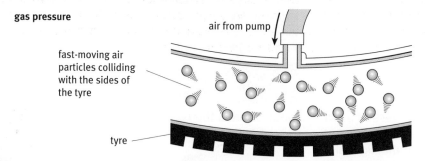

gas pressure

air from pump

fast-moving air particles colliding with the sides of the tyre

tyre

Temperature and heat

Temperature is a measure of how **hot** an object is and is measured in °C (degrees Celsius) or K (kelvin). For example, the temperature of water when it is boiling is 100 °C. The temperature of ice when it is melting is 0 °C. We use a thermometer to measure the temperature of an object.

The heat or **thermal energy** of an object is the energy an object contains because of its temperature. It is measured in joules (J). Heat energy flows from regions of high temperature to regions of lower temperature, that is, from hot to cold.

Transpiration

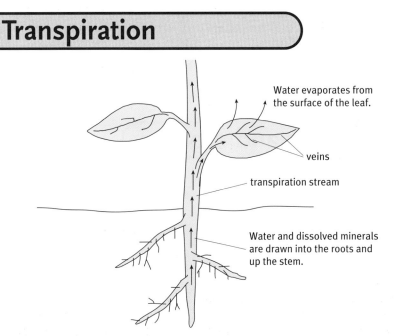

Water evaporates from the surface of the leaf.

veins

transpiration stream

Water and dissolved minerals are drawn into the roots and up the stem.

Loss of water from the leaves of a plant by evaporation is called **transpiration**. This loss draws fresh water, and minerals such as nitrates and phosphates, up from the roots and through the stem. The passage of water and minerals up through the plant is called the **transpiration stream**.

Variation and inheritance

There can be large differences between members of a species. These differences are called **variations**. There are two main types of variation.

1 **Discontinuous variation** describes characteristics that are influenced only by genes inherited from the parents (for example, eye colour and blood group). Discontinuous characteristics have distinct categories; for example, eyes are brown or blue; blood groups are A, B, AB or O.

2 **Continuous variation** describes characteristics that are influenced by genes inherited from the parents *and* also by the conditions of upbringing. Continuous characteristics do not have distinct categories but can have many different values. Height and weight are examples of continuous variation.

Plants and animals can be selectively bred in an attempt to produce offspring with certain desirable characteristics, for example, a rose that has a bright colour might be cross-bred with a rose that has a strong scent in order to produce a rose that has both a bright colour and a strong scent.

Weathering and erosion

All rocks on the surface of the Earth change because of the effects of water, wind, plants and chemicals. This process is called **weathering**.

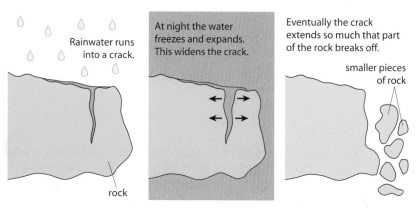

Rainwater runs into a crack.

At night the water freezes and expands. This widens the crack.

Eventually the crack extends so much that part of the rock breaks off.

smaller pieces of rock

rock

Erosion is the moving of rocks and soils by water, wind and gravity.